Tip

Remember to secure the ends of the horizontal strips to hold them in place before weaving the vertical strips.

by Patti Behan

Kevin

MATERIALS: *Paper Garden* (Cactus, Oak Leaf and Stormy Sky cardstock, Cream vellum) • *Creating Keepsakes* Bella font

TIP: Tear edges of cardstock and vellum for photo and font backgrounds.

Really Simple... Basic Weaving

"How do I scrapbook all my portrait proofs?" is a common question. Here's the answer. Woven title and torn paper photo backgrounds are easy, yet elegant, and a great way to showcase your favorite photos!

1. Choose one dark and one light color sheet of cardstock. Cut four ½" strips from light and 3 from dark using a paper trimmer. Cut 2 dark, 3 light strips into thirds.

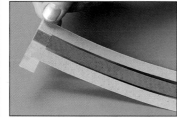

2. Place light, dark and light strips horizontally, and tape to secure the strips.

3. Weave strips that were cut in thirds over and under horizontal strips. Alternate the colors.

4. Repeat for 7 light and 6 dark strips. Trim dark strips as shown. Your piece will look like this.

Tips

• Try cutting strips with wavy edge scissors or decorative rotary blades for a different look.
• Embellish cut out shapes by cutting slits and weaving.

Payleigh getting ready for the Easter Egg Hunt at Aunt Maureen's house.
Easter Sunday
March 31, 2002

A delicate, floral page lets your little darling bloom!

by Jackie McLaughlin

Floral Page

MATERIALS: Pale Pink cardstock • *Anna Griffin* paper (floral, Pink print, large Pink check) • Pop dots • *Creating Keepsakes* oval journalette with Lucida Sans font

TIPS: Cut slits in floral paper and weave with Pink print paper. Print and cut out journaling.

Add Extra Special Dimension with Raised Flowers

1. Cut flower motifs from an extra sheet of print paper.

2. Attach pop dots to the back of the flowers.

3. Center flower over a matching flower and press in place.

Helpful Tip

Choose a sheet of paper for background. Cut slits across the page with the smaller mosaic template.

by Jackie McLaughlin

Jackie & John
MATERIALS: *Anna Griffin* paper (Red/Pink floral stripe, Red/Pink floral, Red/Cream print, Red cardstock, Cream cardstock) • Chatterbox Journaling Genie font
TIPS: Weave the photo mat with Red/Cream print and Red/Pink floral papers. Mount photo on Red cardstock.

Jackie and John
December 23, 2001

Helpful Tips

For the best weaving results, use a sharp swivel knife when cutting paper strips with templates. Or measure carefully and cut with a paper trimmer.

Use extra strips to weave a photo mat. Try cutting strips with decorative scissors or wavy rulers for a different look.

MATERIALS: 3 coordinating sheets of paper • *EZ2Cut* Mosaic Templates • Swivel knife • *3M* Photo Fix Mounting Squares

Basic Background Weaving

Paper weaving gives you the opportunity to make an extra-special layout to highlight your favorite photos and a great way to dress up a single photo!

1. Choose a sheet of paper for background. Cut slits across the page with the smaller mosaic template.

2. Using larger template, cut strips from other sheets of paper.

3. Weave strips over and under through background pages, alternating different papers.

No matter what the theme, woven paper makes each page extraordinary. So, gather your supplies and begin making your own very special memory scrapbook pages.

You are sure to find some wonderful creative paper weaving ideas that will help you to get your own creative juices flowing.

by Jackie McLaughlin

Happy Mother's Day - MATERIALS: Paper Garden *cardstock* (Mauve fiber, Augusta Green fiber) • *Autumn Leaves* print papers (White bow, Aqua ribbon) • Scallop scissors • *Creating Keepsakes* tulip journalette with Bella font

TIPS: Add the narrow strips of Pink cardstock to the weaving. Trim journalette with scallop scissors.

Background Weaving

Helpful Tip

Add extra thin strips of paper to the weave.

by Jackie McLaughlin

Cinco de Mayo - MATERIALS: *Paper Garden* paper (Cornflower Blue cardstock, Sun, Strawberry and Mango vellum) • Primary color fibers • *2 Grrrls* flower and letter stickers • Pop dots • ⅛" circle punch • Large eye needle
TIPS: Mount photo on cardstock. Punch holes around the edge and sew fiber. Weave additional fiber through top and bottom of woven background, glue to secure.

Helpful Tip

Vary the width and number of strips to make the desired size project.

by Jackie McLaughlin

Backyard Concert
MATERIALS: *Paper Garden* cardstock (Cobalt Blue, Orchid, White) • *Punch Bunch* Cornflower Blue and Grape music note die-cuts • *Fiskars* Shape Cutter oval template • *Magic Matter* • *Fiskars* Shape cutter • Black fine tip marker
TIPS: Silhouette several photos and add mats using a Magic Matter to make identical shapes. Cut ovals using a template.

A Magic Matter consists of metal disks that allow you to cut mats in any shape. The disks are ⅛", ¼", ⅜" and ½" in size with a center hole for a pencil tip. You can create mats that change in size uniformly larger or smaller than cut-outs or templates.

Woven Baskets

Woven baskets are a nice way to highlight photos of your child growing up. You could title them 'My, how you've blossomed'. Baskets are perfect additions to gift albums!

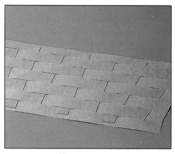

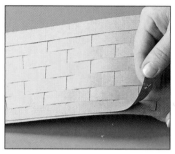

1. Weave eight ½" strips vertically into the basket and space equally. Trim as shown on front and back. Glue loose edges of strips on front and back.

2. Glue 1" strip on top of basket and trim edges. Trim last ½" strip to 7¾". Glue strip on bottom of basket. Place a brad ¾" from each end.

3. Chalk the edges of the strips with 2 shades of Brown chalk.

by Jackie McLaughlin

Hoppy Easter
MATERIALS: *Paper Garden* cardstock (Purple, Electric Pink, Emerald, Bright Blue, Pink) • 10 assorted 4mm rhinestones • *EK Success* Wacky lower case letter template • Craft knife • Pink and Purple gel pens
TIPS: Use gel pens to stitch the letters and decorate the egg. Glue rhinestones on egg.

Emily's Bridal Shower June 9, 2002

by Patti Behan

Blooming Basket
MATERIALS: *Paper Garden* cardstock (Blue Jay, Kraft, Bright Blue, Fuchsia, Bright Canary, Black, Grass Green) • *Accu-Cut* butterfly die-cuts (Blue, Pink, Black) • *Puzzle Mates* Petal Pushers template for leaf and five-petal flowers • *Fiskars* flower and circle templates • 2 Gold brads • Craft knife • Chalk (Blue, Orange, Green, Brown, Tan, Lavender) • Black fine tip pen
TIPS: Cut photos into circles and mat for flower centers. Carefully arrange and glue bouquet.

BASKET PATTERN

Cut slits along lines. Weave $1/2$" strips vertically.

Trace Basket pattern on $8^{1}/_{2}$" x 11" sheet of cardstock and cut out.
Place cut out basket on self-healing mat and cut slits.
Using a 12" paper trimmer, cut nine $1/2$" strips and one 1" strip from another sheet of cardstock for weaving.

Woven Card

Weave a special message for any holiday!

by Jackie McLaughlin

Be Mine
MATERIALS: *Paper Garden* White cardstock • *Ellison* Tomato cupid die-cuts • *EZ2Cut* 1¼" letter template • Swivel knife • Red chalk
TIP: Chalk White strips with Red before weaving.

Woven Basket Pattern

Materials and photo on page 12.

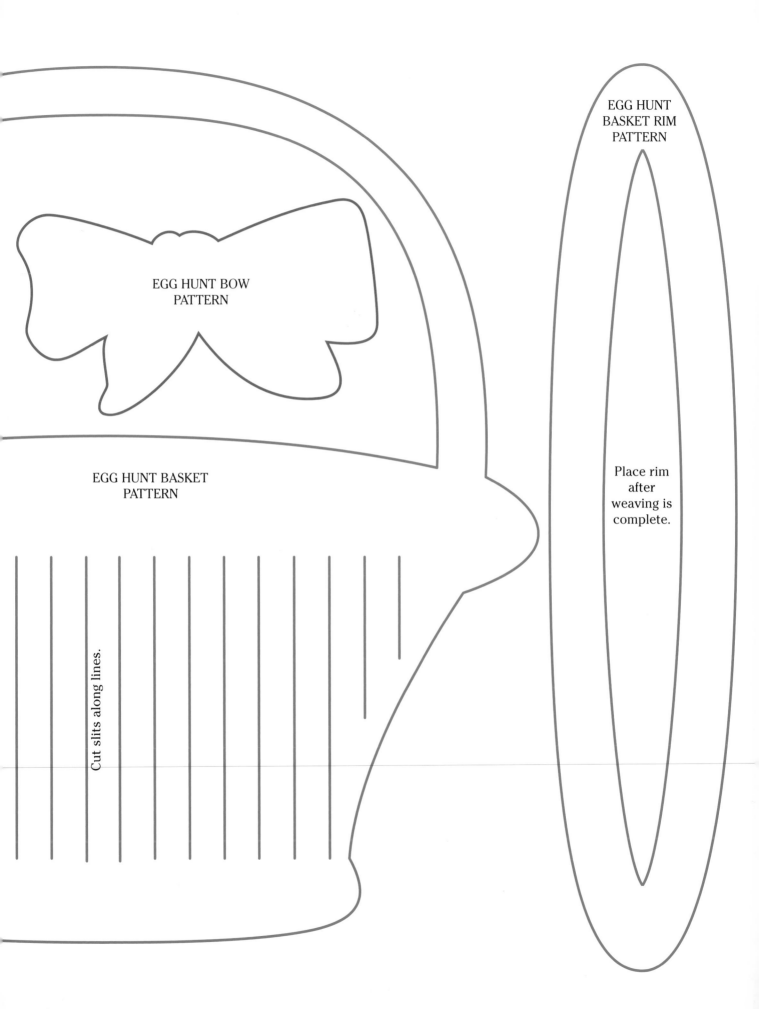

EGG HUNT BASKET RIM
PATTERN

Place rim
after
weaving is
complete.

EGG HUNT BOW
PATTERN

EGG HUNT BASKET
PATTERN

Cut slits along lines.

by Patti Behan

Egg Hunt

MATERIALS: *Paper Garden* cardstock (Bright Blue, Cream, Salmon, Baby Green, Cherry, Canary Yellow) • *Pulsar Paper* Green raffia • Punches (*All Night Media* ¼" star and ½" heart, *EK Success* circle and asterisk) • Oval and 1¼" letter templates • Wavy and zig zag edge rulers • Craft knife • Pink and Grey chalk • Black fine tip pen

TIP: Make egg decorations with punches and rulers.

Helpful Tip

For a finished look, wrap the horizontal strips around to the back and glue in place.

OVAL &
EGG
PATTERNS

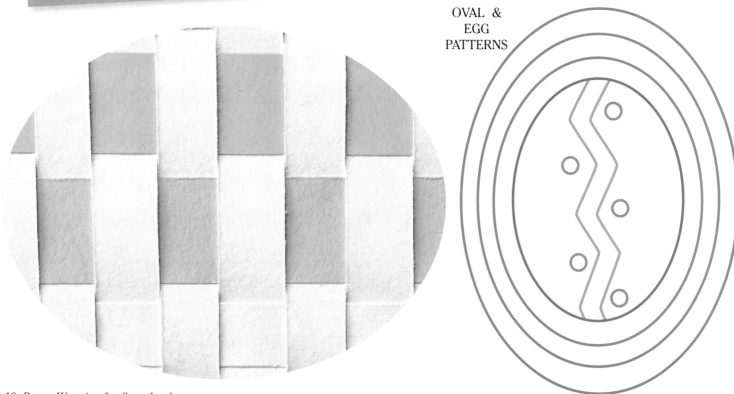

Framed Weaving

Give your scrapbook pages that finished look. Place paper frames around woven pieces for great backgrounds, borders and title strips. This technique is great for card covers too!

by Jackie McLaughlin

Snowing - MATERIALS: *Paper Garden* cardstock (Grey fiber, Pepper fiber, Blueberry fiber, Midnight Sky, Persian Blue) • *Accu-Cut* Marshmallow letter template • *Punch Bunch* 1" and 1¼" snowflake punches • *Fiskars* 12" Paper trimmer • White gel pen
TIP: Add journaling with a White gel pen.

How To Frame

MATERIALS: ¼" strips of cardstock for weaving • Four ⅝" strips of cardstock to finish frame • *EK Success* Glass Mat

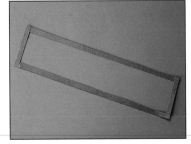

1. Place 4 paper strips on mat to form a rectangle frame and glue strips together.

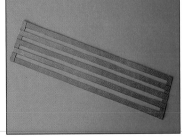

2. Glue 3 strips equally spaced horizontally on frame.

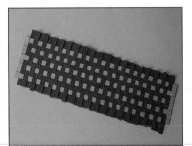

3. Weave remaining ¼" strips until border is complete.

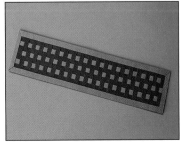

4. Glue ⅝" strips on ends of frame leaving corners unglued.

5. Miter corners. Trim excess and glue corners down.

Helpful Tip

You can vary the number of strips, the size of the frame and use different colors to create additional patterns.

by Patti Behan

Portrait of a Lady - MATERIALS: *Paper Garden* paper (Mauve fiber, Pepper fiber and Black cardstock, Blush and Cream vellum) • *Hot Off the Press* rose print paper • *Accu-Cut* Pink fiber and Grey fiber heart die-cuts • 6 Pink flower eyelets • Eyelet setter • $1/8$" circle punch • *Creating Keepsakes* Bella font
TIPS: Print title on vellum. Attach vellum strips with eyelets.

by Jackie McLaughlin

It's a Girl - MATERIALS: *Paper Garden* cardstock (White, Baby Pink) • *JewelCraft* True Love and Red Hot beads • *Fiskars* Shape Cutter (Victorian & cloud border) • *Creating Keepsakes* Fill In font • 3L double-sided photo tape
TIPS: Fill in letters and make border with beads.

Ice Cream
MATERIALS: *Paper Garden* cardstock (Sedona Gold, Baby Green, Black) • Brown and Green chalk

Helpful Tip

Embellish cut-out shapes by cutting slits and weaving.

Heart - MATERIALS: *Paper Garden* Black cardstock • *Accu-Cut* Woven Heart die-cut (Mauve fiber, Pepper fiber)

Die-Cuts & Paper Piecing with Weaving

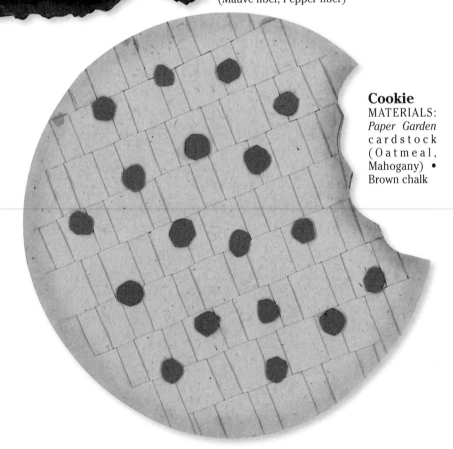

Cookie
MATERIALS: *Paper Garden* cardstock (Oatmeal, Mahogany) • Brown chalk

Woven strips add a new dimension and a whole new realm of visual interest to die-cut shapes.

Use these great ideas to create more visual interest in your scrapbook pages. You'll be proud to show off your works of art!

by Patti Behan

Sunflower - MATERIALS: *Paper Garden* cardstock (Army Green, Charcoal Brown, Evergreen) • *Sizzix* Bright Canary leaf and stem die-cuts

TIPS: Fringe edge of Army Green circle. Hand-cut Evergreen leaves.

by Patti Behan

Pineapple - MATERIALS: *Paper Garden* cardstock (Pumpkin, Forest Green) • Chalk (Brown, Green, White)

by Jackie McLaughlin

St. Patrick's Day - MATERIALS: *Paper Garden* cardstock (Grass Green, Apple Green, Forest Green) • *Punch Bunch* clover punch • *Wordsworth* Chunky letter template • Craft knife

LEAF
PATTERN

by Patti Behan

Acorn - MATERIALS: *Paper Garden* cardstock (Charcoal Brown, Kraft) • Brown chalk

by Patti Behan

Hot Air Balloon
MATERIALS: *Paper Garden* cardstock (Bright Canary, Bright Red, Cobalt, Black) • Wavy ruler • Craft knife

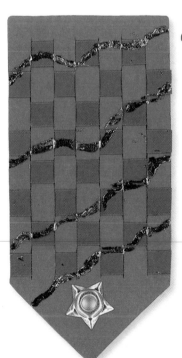

by Patti Behan

Corn
MATERIALS: *Paper Garden* cardstock (Evergreen, Bright Canary)

Tip
Try cutting strips with decorative scissors or rotary blades for a different look.

by Jackie McLaughlin

Christmas Tag
MATERIALS: *Paper Garden* Evergreen cardstock • *Sizzix* Christmas Red tag die-cut • Gold star eyelet • Eyelet setter • 1/8" circle punch • Gold foil

Die-Cuts & Paper Piecing with Weaving

Here's a new and simple way to embellish your die-cuts. Just cut slits in shapes and weave strips horizontally, vertically or even diagonally. Use chalk for added dimension.

A brother is
someone you
you can lean on.
Timmy & Kevin
Summer 1993

Here is the answer to all your border requirements. Weave borders to match any season or theme.

by Jackie McLaughlin

Brothers

MATERIALS: *Paper Garden* (Navy linen, Blue Stone and Sky Blue marble cardstock, vellum) • *Ellison* Navy linen baby buggy die-cut • *Fiskars* Oval-1 border template • 4 Silver and 2 White eyelets • Eyelet setter • ⅛" circle punch • *EZ2Cut* mosaic template & swivel knife • *Creating Keepsakes* Journaling font

TIP: Attach journaling and baby buggy with eyelets.

by Patti Behan

Oriental Border

MATERIALS: *Paper Garden* cardstock (Christmas Red, Black) • *All Night Media* dragon and pagoda punches • Glue pen

TIPS: Cut ⅞" strips of Red and ¼" strips of Red for weaving. Add punched shapes.

by Patti Behan

Southwest Border

MATERIALS: *Paper Garden* cardstock (Pumpkin, Sea Blue, Chili, Brick) • *Fiskars* shape template • *EK Success* punches (diamond, Kokopelli) • Craft knife • Glue pen

TIP: Use shape template to cut border and add punched designs.

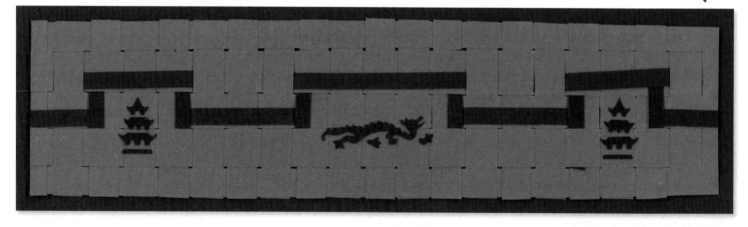

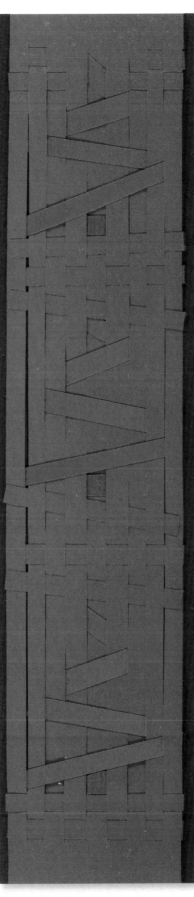

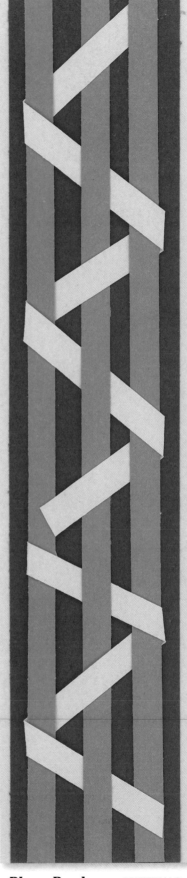

Tip

• For the best weaving results, use a sharp craft knife when cutting paper strips with templates. Or measure carefully and cut with a paper trimmer.

• Remember to secure the ends of the horizontal strips to hold them in place before weaving the vertical strips.

• Try cutting strips with decorative scissors or rotary blades for a different look.

Star Border - MATERIALS: *Paper Garden* cardstock (White, Christmas Red, Persian Blue, Pepper fiber, Midnight Sky) • *Robin's Nest* raffia (Red, White, Blue)
TIP: Cut 6" piece of raffia, tie knot in center and glue on stars.

Tree Border - MATERIALS: *Paper Garden* cardstock (Christmas Red, Grass Green, Brown, Gold Pearl)
TIP: Weave design with ¼" strips and glue on Gold background.

Blue Border - MATERIALS: *Paper Garden* cardstock (Bright Blue, Marine Blue, Baby Blue)
TIP: Weave design with ⅜" strips.

and... more Fun Stuff!

by Jackie McLaughlin

Holidays and special occasions call for special page accents. Have fun!

Pumpkins Border

MATERIALS: *Paper Garden* cardstock (Desert Sky, Marigold) • *ScripScraps* Terra Cotta paper • *Fiskars* Victorian border template • *Accu-Cut* Orange and Brown pumpkin die-cuts • Craft knife • *Creating Keepsakes* Topper font • Brown chalk • Brown fine tip pen

TIPS: Cut out strips for weaving with template. Cut around title to shape.

Thanksgiving Border

MATERIALS: *Paper Garden* cardstock (Desert Sky, Marigold, Tangerine, Electric Orange, Buckeye, Terra Cotta, Burnt Orange, Desert Tan, Mahogany, Charcoal Brown) • *Punch Bunch* small punches (maple leaf, oak leaf, impatiens) • *Sizzix* Fun Serif 'Thanksgiving'

TIPS: Weave Desert Sky background with ¼" strips of Marigold and Tangerine. Punch shapes from remaining cardstock colors.

It's a Boy
MATERIALS: *Paper Garden* cardstock (Denim, Blue Granite fiber, Dusk) • *Punch Bunch* teddy bear punch • *Fiskars* Scallop border template • Brush script font • *Magic Matter* • EZ2Cut Mosaic template • Swivel knife

TIP: Make a mat for the teddy bear using the Magic Matter with 1/8" disk.

Merry Christmas
MATERIALS: *Paper Garden* cardstock (Tomato, Evergreen, Gold Pearl) • *Adept Innovations* eA-Zy 'Merry Christmas' punch letter set • *All Night Media* punches (Santa hat, tree) • EZ2Cut Mosaic template & swivel knife

TIP: Weave design with 3/8" strips.

Boo - MATERIALS: *Paper Garden* cardstock (Bright Orange, Violet, Black) • *Ellison* Violet ghost die-cut • *Accu-Cut* Marshmallow letter template • *Fiskars* diamond border template • Craft knife

TIPS: Weave strips made with diamond border. Mat letters and ghost with Black.

New Year's Eve - MATERIALS: *Paper Garden* cardstock (Pepper fiber, Grey fiber) • *Sizzix* Black Fun Serif upper case and confetti die-cuts • *Scrapyard 329* Silver metal embellishments • EZ2Cut Mosaic template & Swivel knife

TIP: Attach metal embellishments to highlight Black letters.

School Days - MATERIALS: *Paper Garden* cardstock (Tomato, Gold, Grass Green, Black, Silver Pearl, Canary Yellow) • EZ2Cut letter template • *Punch Bunch* small apple punch • EZ2Cut Mosaic template & swivel knife • *EK Success* pencil stencil • Craft knife

TIPS: Place apple shapes in letter openings. Draw pencil shapes using template, cut out and assemble.

Cane Weaving with Cardstock

by Patti Behan

The age old look of caning is easy to achieve with simple paper strips and a Glass Mat.

Follow the easy step-by-step instructions and you'll have an intricate background in minutes. Use the caned pieces for photo mats, pockets or pages.

Whee! Roller Coaster Fun!

Josh
MATERIALS: *Paper Garden* cardstock (Black, Christmas Red, Silver Pearl) • *Making Memories* Grey stripe paper • *Accu-Cut* Jill's Chunky alphabet die-cut letters • Craft knife
TIP: Make a caned background for the photo and add narrow strips of Christmas Red cardstock to accent the letter blocks.

Roller Coaster
MATERIALS: *Paper Garden* cardstock (Bright Blue, Black, Smoke, Silver Pearl) • *Accu-Cut* Tomato roller coaster car die-cut • *Sizzix* dolls, hair and clothes die-cuts (Yellow, Flesh, Black, Red and Brown cardstock, *Paper Patch* Yellow dot and plaid paper) • *All Night Media* lightning bolt and 1/4" circle punches • White gel pen
TIPS: Hand-cut girl's ponytail. Draw wheel details with gel pen.

MATERIALS: Seventy ⅛" strips of 12" cardstock • Eight ¼" strips of 12" cardstock • EK Success Glass Mat™ • Invisible tape

1. Place two ⅛" strips vertically in one grid block of the Glass Mat. Tape in place. Skip 2 grid blocks and place 2 more strips. Repeat 2 more times.

2. Weave ⅛" strips horizontally. Start on right and weave over and under each vertical strip. With the next strip, go under and over. Skip 2 grid blocks, repeat as far down as you can. Realign strips with grid blocks as you weave so the finished project is straight.

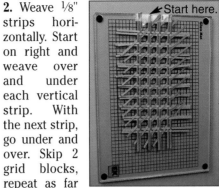

3. First Diagonal Weave - Starting a top left, find the second set of vertical strips and weave under and over horizontal strips. Find the next group of vertical strips and repeat all the way down.

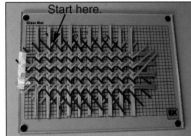

Tip
Use craft tweezers to help with the diagonal weaving.

4. Second Diagonal Weave - Turn mat 90° so taped strips are on your right. Find the second set of vertical strips on top left and start weaving horizontally under vertical strips and over horizontal strips until you reach the end.

5. Finish Edges: Glue the ¼" strips down with a glue pen on the outside sets of strips leaving the corners unglued for mitering.

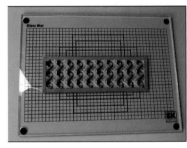

6. Miter Corners - With small scissors make a cut on the diagonal where the corners meet. Take out loose pieces. Glue down corners. Glue remaining ¼" strips down on back. There is no need to miter strips on the back. Trim edges.

Report Card
MATERIALS: *Paper Garden* cardstock (Bright Blue, Christmas Red, Marine Blue) • *Mrs. Grossman's* school stickers • Assorted photos and report cards • Black marker
TIPS: Weave a framed cane pocket and glue 3 sides on page. Make title with cardstock, stickers and marker.

Add stickers to your pages for an intricate hand-painted look you can achieve in seconds!

The Graduate
MATERIALS: *Paper Garden* paper (Cookies & Cream, Champagne Stone, Forest Green and Buff cardstock, Turf and Forest Green vellum) • Ivy rub-on • Brush script MT computer font for title • Yellow chalk • *Creating Keepsakes* Cursive font • Craft knife
TIP: Rub ivy on clear vellum and cut out for border decoration.

Borders with Cane Weaving

by Patti Behan

Try making caned borders using different colored strips in a variety of combinations. These borders do not really need embellishment… the different color combinations look great! But, of course, they do look wonderful with letters, stickers or die-cuts! This technique would be fantastic for the front of a greeting card!

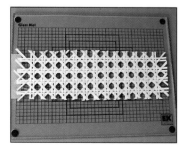

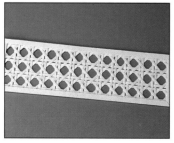

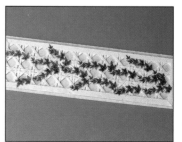

1. Weave a caned border following instructions on page 23.

2. Add a frame and miter the corners.

3. Add stickers to decorate.

4. Add die-cut or sticker letters for titles.

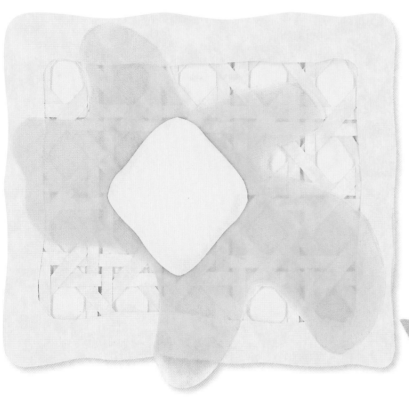

Paper Piecing with Cane Weaving

Waffle - MATERIALS: *Paper Garden* paper (Champagne Stone and Ivory cardstock, vellum) • Beige chalk
TIP: Hand-cut vellum syrup shape and color with chalk.

Chair
MATERIALS: *Paper Garden* cardstock (Tan, Desert Tan) • *Anna Griffin* rose print paper

Weaving with paper is a fabulous way to add texture and dimension to your scrapbook pages.

Borders

It is so much fun to make caned borders that you'll want to try them in an infinite variety of colors.

Helpful Tip

For the best weaving results, use a sharp craft knife when cutting paper strips with templates. Or measure carefully and cut with a paper trimmer.

by Patti Behan

Summertime Border
MATERIALS: *Paper Garden* cardstock (Electric Pink, Lime Green, Grass Green)

by Ann Uliano

Senior Prom
MATERIALS: *Paper Garden* cardstock (Cookies & Cream, Green fiber, Green) • *Making Memories* Green print paper • *Sandy Lion* flower and ivy stickers • Computer generated journaling
TIPS: Print journaling in a color to match background paper. Arrange and apply climbing ivy on border.

Titles with Cane Weaving

Make outstanding title strips with caning! You'll be surprised at the beautiful results.

Blue Caned Border
MATERIALS: *Paper Garden* cardstock (Blue Moon, Cornflower Blue, Persian Blue)

by Patti Behan

Allstar
MATERIALS: *Paper Garden* cardstock (Midnight Sky, Bright Blue, Christmas Red, Mahogany) • *Hot Off the Press* baseball paper • *Pulsar Paper* Natural raffia • *Artistic* 26 gauge Blue wire • *Sizzix* Fun Serif baseball print letter die-cuts • *Accu-Cut* White baseball die-cut • *Fiskars* star and circle templates • 1/16" circle punch • Craft knife • White gel pen • Grey chalk • Markers (Black, Blue Red)
TIPS: Hand cut bat. Punch holes in star and bat and attach with wire, curling ends to secure.

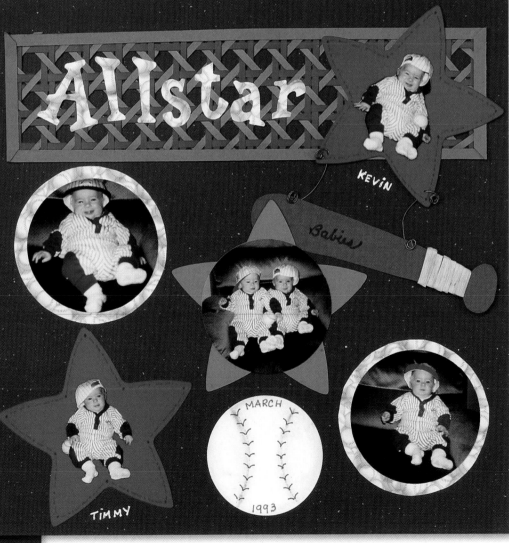

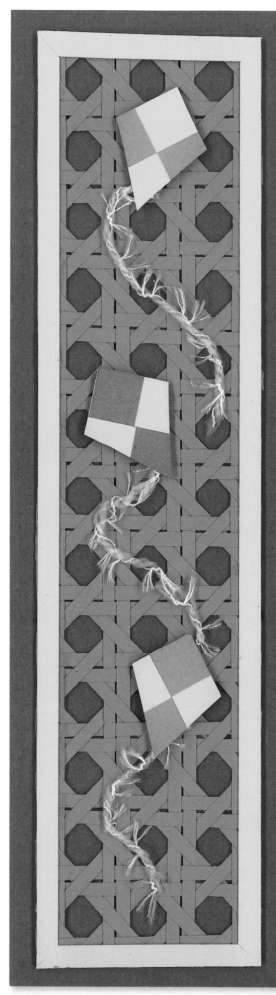

Cane Borders & Titles

Decorate your caned borders with small die-cuts and punch art for a fun or elegant look.

by Patti Behan

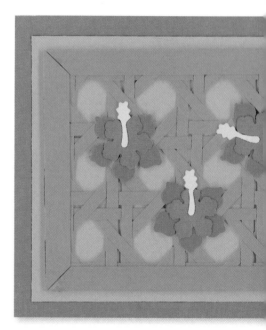

Cornucopia Border
MATERIALS: *Paper Garden* cardstock (Desert Sky, Marigold, Buckeye, Bright Orange, Mahogany, Electric Orange, Evergreen, Gold, Pumpkin) • *Accu-Cut* Mahogany cornucopia die-cut • 1" circle punch • Orange chalk • Black fine tip marker
TIP: Hand cut leaves, squash and stems.

Kite Border
MATERIALS: *Paper Garden* cardstock (Bright Blue, Bright Canary, Marine Blue, Bright Red) • White fiber • Mini glue dots
TIPS: Use fiber for kite strings. Attach kites with glue dots.

Aloha Border
MATERIALS: *Paper Garden* cardstock (Emerald Green, Electric Green, Bright Blue, Bright Canary, Bright Red) • Punches (*All Night Media* hibiscus, *EK Success* lotus) • *Sizzix* Fun Serif upper and lower case Bright Blue letter die-cuts

Grapevine Border
MATERIALS: *Paper Garden* cardstock (Cookies & Cream, Pepper fiber, Steel Blue, Violet, Forest Green, Mahogany) • *Sizzix* Buckeye ivy die-cuts • Punches (grape leaf, ¼" and ½" circle) • Purple chalk
TIP: Stack and glue circles to make grape clusters.